RANA KUMBHA

MAHARANA MOKAL, THE RULER OF MEWAR, WAS CAMPING AT BAGOR (NEAR CHITTOR) WHILE ON A TOUR OF HIS KINGDOM. ONE QUIET AFTERNOON THE RANA WAS RESTING IN HIS TENT.

NOT FAR AWAY, TWO OF HIS OFFICERS, THE BROTHERS CHACHA AND MERA, WERE CONSPIRING WITH ANOTHER OFFICER, MAHPA, TO MURDER HIM.

MAHPA, THE RANA HAS INSULTED US. SOME TIME AGO, IN THE PRESENCE OF ALL THE CHIEFS, HE POINTED TO A TREE AND ASKED ME WHAT IT WAS CALLED.

HE WANTED TO REMIND US THAT OUR GRANDFATHER WAS A CARPENTER.

HE SHALL PAY WITH HIS LIFE.

WE SHALL AVENGE THIS INSULT.

YOU HAVE MY SUPPORT.

LOOKING FOR FURTHER SUPPORT, THE THREE MEN ASKED MALESI, THE RANA'S CHIEF GUARD, TO JOIN THEM. BUT THE LOYAL GUARD INFORMED THE RANA OF THE CONSPIRACY.

... AND NOW CHACHA AND MERA HAVE WON THE SUPPORT OF MAHPA. WE MUST BE ON OUR GUARD.

THE RANA DID NOT TAKE THE WARNING SERIOUSLY.

CHACHA AND MERA? WE CAN TAKE CARE OF THEM WITH EASE! BUT I DON'T THINK THEY WILL DARE TO RISE AGAINST ME.

HE WAS WRONG. THE VERY NEXT DAY, THE CONSPIRATORS DECIDED TO STRIKE. AS THEY RODE TOWARDS THE RANA'S TENT IT WAS PRINCE KUMBHA WHO ALERTED THE RANA.

FATHER! CHACHA AND MERA ARE COMING WITH THEIR MEN.

QUICK! BRING MY WEAPONS.

EVEN AS RANA MOKAL AND THE OTHERS GOT READY...

...THE CONSPIRATORS ENTERED THE TENT.

TRAITORS! IS THIS HOW YOU REPAY YOUR BENEFACTOR!

YOU INSULT US IN PUBLIC AND THEN CALL YOURSELF OUR BENEFACTOR! CHARGE, MERA! GET TO WORK, MAHPA!

THE RANA DREW HIS SWORD AND . . .

. . . HIS BLADE CLASHED WITH THOSE OF THE TRAITORS.

RANI HADI * BRAVELY ENTERED THE FRAY.

BUT THE RUTHLESS CONSPIRATORS SHOWED HER NO MERCY. WHEN SHE FELL, THE RANA CRIED OUT TO HIS YOUNG SON —

KUMBHA! FLEE! WASTE NO TIME!

I CAN'T LEAVE YOU, FATHER! I'LL FIGHT WITH YOU.

* KUMBHA'S STEP-MOTHER

4

5

INSIDE THE TENT —
THE RANA IS DEAD. BUT HIS SON STILL LIVES.

WE'LL GO AFTER HIM.

MEANWHILE, KUMBHA HAD FLED TO A PATEL'S* HOUSE NEAR BY.

THE RANA HAS BEEN MURDERED. I NEED A HORSE TO TAKE ME TO CHITTOR.

THE PATEL QUICKLY TOOK HIM TO HIS STABLES.

THESE TWO HORSES ARE THE FASTEST IN MEWAR. THEY ARE YOURS.

I WILL TAKE ONE. BUT FIRST I MUST MAKE SURE THAT NO ONE TAKES THE OTHER HORSE TO COME AFTER ME.

* VILLAGE CHIEF

THEY BURST INTO THE PATEL'S STABLE.

WE HAVE BEEN FORESTALLED! KUMBHA HAS KILLED THE SECOND HORSE.

COME, LET'S NOT WASTE ANY TIME. WE MUST CAPTURE KUMBHA BEFORE HE REACHES CHITTOR.

BUT KUMBHA HAD ALREADY REACHED CHITTOR.

CLOSE THE GATES! BE QUICK!

WE ARE TOO LATE! KUMBHA HAS ESCAPED.

NEVER MIND. WE'LL GET HIM SOME OTHER TIME.

LATER, KUMBHA WAS CROWNED RANA OF CHITTOR.

AFTER THE CORONATION, KUMBHA CONFERRED WITH HIS GRANDMOTHER, HANSA BAI.

MAHPA, CHACHA AND MERA ARE STILL AT LARGE. I MUST PURSUE THEM.

NO, KUMBHA! DON'T LEAVE CHITTOR TILL YOU HAVE CONSOLIDATED YOUR POSITION. SEND WORD TO MY BROTHER WHO WILL CERTAINLY HELP YOU.

KUMBHA SENT AN ENVOY TO RAO RAN MAL, THE RATHOD KING OF MARWAR.

RANA MOKAL HAS BEEN MURDERED! I BOW MY HEAD IN SHAME FOR NOT PREVENTING THIS.

9

HE TOOK OFF HIS TURBAN AND THREW IT TO THE GROUND.

I VOW NOT TO WEAR A PUGRI TILL THIS FOUL DEED IS AVENGED.

THEREAFTER, HE BEGAN WEARING A PHENTA—A SIMPLE HEAD-DRESS.

RAO RAN MAL THEN WENT TO CHITTOR.

THE TREACHEROUS ASSAULT ON RANA MOKAL BURNS MY HEART . . .

. . . AND A VOLCANO ERUPTS IN EVERY FIBRE OF MY BEING.

RAO RAN MAL SET OUT TOWARDS THE PAI KOTRA HILLS WHERE THE TRAITORS WERE HIDING.

WHEN HE REACHED THE FOOT OF THE HILLS, HE ASKED THE BHILS, THE TRIBALS OF THE AREA, FOR INFORMATION ABOUT THE TRAITORS.

YOUR MAJESTY, IT IS TRUE THEY ARE HIDING IN THE FORT. BUT WAIT FOR A FEW DAYS. A LIONESS HAS JUST GIVEN BIRTH TO A CUB AND THE PATH IS BLOCKED.

I CAN'T WAIT. I MUST START CLIMBING THE HILL AT ONCE.

RAO RAN MAL BEGAN THE HAZARDOUS CLIMB WITH SIXTY TRUSTED MEN.

AS THE PARTY REACHED A LEDGE OF ROCK—

IT IS THE LIONESS!

RAN MAL'S SON JUMPED FORWARD...

...AND BEFORE THE LIONESS COULD ATTACK..

...HE BURIED HIS DAGGER INTO HER HEART.

THE PARTY SOON REACHED THE SUMMIT. RAO RAN MAL'S SOLDIERS SCRAMBLED OVER THE PARAPET.

JUST THEN, THE DRUMMER ACCOMPANYING RAO RAN MAL'S ARMY SLIPPED AND...

...HIS DRUM FELL DOWN...

...WITH A RE-SOUNDING CRASH.

INSIDE THE FORT, CHACHA'S DAUGHTER WOKE UP WITH A START.

FATHER! DID YOU HEAR THAT? PERHAPS KUMBHA'S MEN ARE HERE!

IT'S ONLY THE SOUND OF THUNDER! GO TO SLEEP, CHILD. KUMBHA'S MEN WON'T DARE TO CLIMB THIS STEEP HILL.

BUT SUDDENLY—

FATHER!

CHACHA WHIRLED ROUND.

RAO RAN MAL! YOU!

YES! I AM HERE TO AVENGE THE MURDER OF RANA MOKAL.

AARGH!

AFTER KILLING CHACHA AND MERA, RAO RAN MAL WENT IN SEARCH OF MAHPA.

HE'S NOT HERE. THE BIRD HAS FLOWN.

THANK GOD! THEY DON'T SUSPECT A THING.

MAHPA ESCAPED IN THE GUISE OF A WOMAN.

RAO RAN MAL RETURNED TO KUMBHA'S PALACE AT CHITTOR.

WE'VE TAKEN CARE OF CHACHA AND MERA. BUT MAHPA CANNOT BE FOUND.

A FEW YEARS LATER A MESSENGER CALLED ON KUMBHA.

YOUR MAJESTY, MAHPA HAS BEEN SEEN IN MANDU.

I'LL ASK SULTAN MAHMUD KHILJI TO RETURN THE CRIMINAL TO US.

SOME TIME LATER, KUMBHA'S ENVOY RETURNED AFTER MEETING THE SULTAN.

YOUR MAJESTY, THE SULTAN SAYS THAT MAHPA IS NOW UNDER HIS PROTECTION AND REFUSES TO SEND HIM BACK.

KUMBHA TURNED TO HIS UNCLE.

IF THE SULTAN WILL NOT SEND MAHPA TO CHITTOR WE WILL GO TO MANDU TO BRING HIM, WON'T WE, UNCLE?

SO RANA KUMBHA AND RAN MAL LEFT CHITTOR WITH THEIR FORCES.

THEY WERE INTERCEPTED NEAR SARANGPUR* BY THE SULTAN'S ARMY.

THE RAJPUTS PUT UP A VERY STRONG FIGHT AND THE SULTAN WAS FORCED TO RETREAT TO THE FORTRESS OF MANDU.

FALL BACK! BACK TO THE FORT!

* SITUATED BETWEEN CHITTOR AND MANDSAUR

THE RAJPUTS PURSUED THE RETREATING ARMY AND LAID SIEGE TO THE FORTRESS OF MANDU.

I WONDER HOW LONG THEY CAN HOLD OUT.

I THINK WE SHOULD ATTACK WITHOUT DELAY.

MEANWHILE, SULTAN MAHMUD KHILJI SENT FOR MAHPA.

MAHPA, I CAN NO LONGER GIVE YOU SHELTER. GO AND SEEK THE RANA'S PARDON.

THE RANA WILL SHOW ME NO MERCY. I'D BETTER ESCAPE.

HE RODE UP TO THE RAMPARTS OF THE FORT...

I ONLY HOPE I WILL NOT BE SPOTTED BY THE RAJPUTS.

MAHMUD KHILJI WAS TAKEN CAPTIVE.

SULTAN, WHERE IS MAHPA?

YOU HAVEN'T FOUND HIM? SO I HAVE THE LAST LAUGH IT APPEARS. YOU HAVE ME, BUT NOT MAHPA!

WE WILL GET HIM YET, IF HE IS STILL ALIVE!*

RANA KUMBHA RETURNED TO CHITTOR IN TRIUMPH.

WE WILL BUILD A PILLAR TO COMMEMORATE OUR VICTORY OVER MAHMUD KHILJI.

SCULPTORS AND SKILLED ARTISANS CAME FROM FAR AND NEAR TO WORK ON THE PILLAR OF VICTORY.

IT'S OUR PRIVILEGE TO WORK FOR RANA KUMBHA.

HE HAS RESTORED THE GLORY OF THE RAJPUTS.

* YEARS LATER, MAHPA SOUGHT AND OBTAINED KUMBHA'S PARDON.

IN 1444, KUMBHA WAS AT HARAVATI PUNISHING SOME REBELS, WHEN HE RECEIVED A MESSAGE FROM CHITTOR.

SULTAN KHILJI'S ARMY IS RANSACK-ING THE OUTSKIRTS OF MEWAR.

I WILL DEAL WITH THE SULTAN AT ONCE.

KUMBHA'S ARMY CAME UPON THE SULTAN'S FORCES NEAR MANDALGARH.

ATTACK!

SULTAN MAHMUD KHILJI WAS ONCE AGAIN DEFEATED BY THE RANA AND HAD TO FLEE.

MEANWHILE, WORK ON THE RANA'S VIC-TORY PILLAR CONTINUED. IT WAS COM-PLETED IN 1448.

* THE FORT BUILT BY KUMBHA ON A HIGH PEAK OF THE WESTERN RANGE OF THE ARAVALI HILLS.

KUMBHA ADVANCED UPON NAGAUR AND STORMED THE FORT.

AS MUJAHID KHAN FLED FOR HIS LIFE...

...KUMBHA ENTERED THE FORT IN TRIUMPH WITH SHAMSKHAN BY HIS SIDE.

KUMBHA PLACED SHAMSKHAN ON THE THRONE.

I AM VERY GRATEFUL TO YOU, MAHARANA. BUT FOR YOUR HELP I WOULD NOT HAVE GOT BACK MY KINGDOM.

KUMBHA MARCHED TO NAGAUR AGAIN AND TOOK THE FORT AFTER DRIVING OUT SHAMSKHAN.

DEMOLISH THE FORTIFICATIONS!

SHAMSKHAN FLED TO AHMEDABAD AND SOUGHT THE HELP OF QUTB-UD-DIN, SULTAN OF GUJARAT.

SHAMSKHAN, I'LL DRIVE KUMBHA OUT OF NAGAUR.

WE MUST MAKE THOROUGH PREPARATIONS. KUMBHA IS NO ORDINARY MILITARY COMMANDER.

THE SULTAN OF GUJARAT SENT HIS SOLDIERS TO NAGAUR, BUT THEY WERE EASILY DEFEATED BY KUMBHA.

25

IT WAS INDEED KUMBHA. HE HAD REACHED KUMBHALGARH BY ANOTHER ROUTE AND HAD COME OUT TO COUNTER THE SULTAN'S ATTACK.

KUMBHA DEFEATED THE SULTAN OF GUJARAT WHO WAS FORCED TO RETRACE HIS STEPS. ON HIS WAY BACK—

SULTAN, I AM TEJ KHAN, THE PRIME MINISTER OF SULTAN KHILJI. IF THE FORCES OF MANDU AND GUJARAT JOIN HANDS, KUMBHA CAN BE EASILY DEFEATED.

I AM PREPARED TO ENTER INTO AN ALLIANCE WITH THE SULTAN OF MANDU.

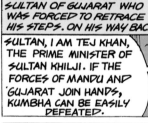

AT CHITTOR —

RANA, THE GUJARAT FORCES ARE ADVANCING TOWARDS KUMBHALGARH. AND MAHMUD KHILJI IS PREPARING TO MARCH TOWARDS CHITTOR. THEY HAVE FORGED AN ALLIANCE AGAINST MEWAR.

PREPARE TO MEET THE GUJA-RAT FORCES FIRST. THE SUL-TAN OF MANDU, TOO, WILL GET A FITTING RECEPTION.

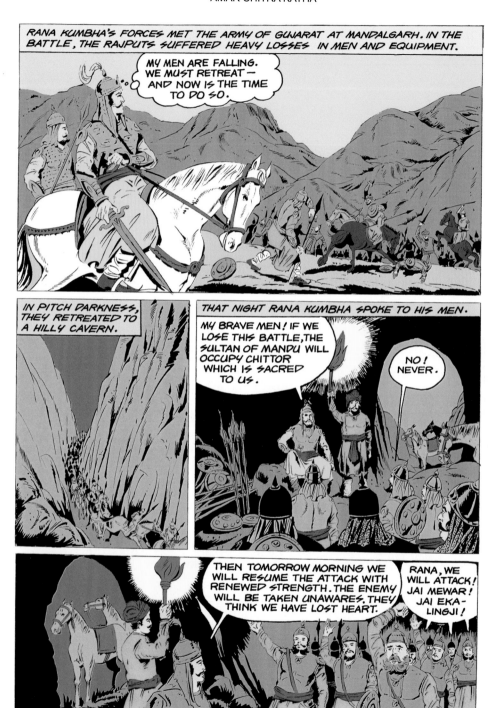

RANA KUMBHA'S FORCES MET THE ARMY OF GUJARAT AT MANDALGARH. IN THE BATTLE, THE RAJPUTS SUFFERED HEAVY LOSSES IN MEN AND EQUIPMENT.

MY MEN ARE FALLING. WE MUST RETREAT — AND NOW IS THE TIME TO DO SO.

IN PITCH DARKNESS, THEY RETREATED TO A HILLY CAVERN.

THAT NIGHT RANA KUMBHA SPOKE TO HIS MEN.

MY BRAVE MEN! IF WE LOSE THIS BATTLE, THE SULTAN OF MANDU WILL OCCUPY CHITTOR WHICH IS SACRED TO US.

NO! NEVER.

THEN TOMORROW MORNING WE WILL RESUME THE ATTACK WITH RENEWED STRENGTH. THE ENEMY WILL BE TAKEN UNAWARES. THEY THINK WE HAVE LOST HEART.

RANA, WE WILL ATTACK! JAI MEWAR! JAI EKA-LINGJI!

BUT HE WAS IN FOR A SURPRISE.

A CLOUD OF DUST IN THE EAST! COULD IT BE...?

OH, IT IS KUMBHA!

THE SURPRISE ATTACK DEMORALISED THE FORCES OF MANDU.

I HAVE TRIED TIME AND AGAIN TO DEFEAT THE RANA. HE IS INVINCIBLE. I HAVE TO ACCEPT THIS BITTER TRUTH.

THEN THE SULTAN OF MANDU CALLED OUT TO HIS MEN.

TURN AROUND, MY MEN! RETREAT!

RANA KUMBHA WATCHED CONTENTEDLY AS THE SULTAN'S ARMY RETREATED.

HE WON'T TROUBLE US AGAIN. BUT EVEN IF HE DOES, WHAT DOES IT MATTER? AS LONG AS OUR PEOPLE ARE VIGILANT, THERE CAN BE NO THREAT TO OUR INDEPENDENCE.

CELEBRATING

50 YEARS

AMAR CHITRA KATHA

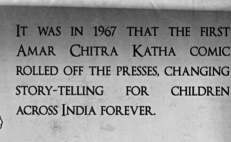

IT WAS IN 1967 THAT THE FIRST AMAR CHITRA KATHA COMIC ROLLED OFF THE PRESSES, CHANGING STORY-TELLING FOR CHILDREN ACROSS INDIA FOREVER.

FIVE DECADES AND MORE THAN 400 BOOKS LATER, WE ARE STILL SHARING STORIES FROM INDIA'S RICH HERITAGE, PRIMARILY BECAUSE OF THE LOVE AND SUPPORT SHOWN BY READERS LIKE YOURSELF.

SO, FROM US TO YOU, HERE'S A BIG

THANK YOU!

RANA PRATAP

The route to your roots

RANA PRATAP

Disdaining even the comfort of a bed, the valiant Rana Pratap waged a single-minded, life-long war against the mighty Mughal conquerors. His Rajput pride instilled a deep respect in the enemy. They realised that huge armies and sophisticated weapons are but aids, and that there can be no substitute for raw courage on the battlefield.

Script
Yagya Sharma

Illustrations
Pratap Mulick

Editor
Anant Pai

Rana Pratap

RAJASTHAN IN WESTERN INDIA WAS THE HOME OF THE VALIANT RAJPUTS.

THROUGHOUT HISTORY, THEY HAD REPEATEDLY FOUGHT FOR THE HONOUR OF THE COUNTRY.

BUT THE RAJPUTS OF CHITTOR SURPASSED ALL, IN DEEDS OF BRAVERY AND PERSONAL SACRIFICE.

IN THE EIGHTH CENTURY A.D. THEY REPULSED AN INVASION OF THEIR LAND.

AND THEIR WOMEN WERE NO LESS HEROIC. CHITTOR'S QUEEN KARMA DEVI HAD DEFEATED THE POWERFUL HORDES OF QUTAB-UD-DIN.

IN THE 14TH CENTURY, QUEEN PADMINI AND HUNDREDS OF RAJPUT WOMEN OF CHITTOR PERFORMED SATI, AN ACT OF SELF-IMMOLATION TO SAVE THEIR HONOUR FROM THE INVADER, ALA-UD-DIN KHILJI.

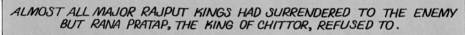

THE MUGHALS WERE THE FIRST INVADERS WHO SUCCEEDED IN OCCUPYING CHITTOR.

ALMOST ALL MAJOR RAJPUT KINGS HAD SURRENDERED TO THE ENEMY BUT RANA PRATAP, THE KING OF CHITTOR, REFUSED TO.

I SWEAR THAT I WILL SACRIFICE MY VERY LIFE FOR CHITTOR.

WE ALSO PLEDGE THAT TILL WE ATTAIN FREEDOM, WE WILL NOT SLEEP ON A BED BUT ON THE GROUND AND WE WILL NOT WEAR FANCY CLOTHES.

MAY GODDESS KALI BLESS YOU RANAJI, YOU HAVE TAKEN A TERRIBLE OATH.

GURUDEV, DEFENDING ONE'S MOTHERLAND IS A SERIOUS MATTER...

... AND NO SACRIFICE IS TOO BIG FOR SUCH A NOBLE CAUSE.

WE WILL FIGHT FOR FREEDOM WITH THE LAST DROP OF OUR BLOOD.

WELL SAID. BUT OUR TASK IS A DIFFICULT ONE. MANY OF OUR OWN PEOPLE ARE HELPING THE INVADERS.

WE MUST INCREASE OUR STRENGTH. LET'S CAPTURE AN IMPORTANT FORT FIRST.

MEANWHILE, IN THE COURT OF AKBAR —

HAVE YOU HEARD THE LATEST JOKE? PRATAP STILL CALLS HIMSELF THE KING OF CHITTOR.

OF COURSE, HE IS A KING BUT WITHOUT A KINGDOM.

SILENCE! YOU FORGET THAT PRATAP HAS TAKEN A FORT.

BUT SIR, OUR HUGE ARMY CAN CRUSH HIM IN NO TIME.

YOU ARE WRONG. IT IS NOT GOING TO BE EASY TO CRUSH PRATAP.

MEANWHILE IN RANA PRATAP'S FORT –

RANAJI! THIS MAN WAS TILLING HIS LAND.

WHY DID YOU DISOBEY MY ORDERS?

BUT I HAD TAKEN THE PERMISSION OF THE MUGHAL GOVERNOR.

I AM THE KING OF CHITTOR AND I HAVE NOT GIVEN YOU THE PERMISSION...

...YOUR CROP WILL FINALLY FEED THE ENEMY AND THUS HELP HIM.

FOR ACTING AGAINST THE INTEREST OF OUR MOTHER-LAND, YOU SHALL DIE!

THE FOLLOWING DAY, THE FARMER WAS HANGED.

THE NEWS OF THE FARMER'S DEATH REACHED AKBAR.

THIS IS OUTRAGEOUS. PERHAPS HE CAN STILL BE WON OVER.

AKBAR CONSULTED HIS RAJPUT COMMANDER, MAN SINGH.

A BRAVE MAN LIKE PRATAP SHOULD BE OUR FRIEND, RAJA MAN SINGH. PLEASE GO AND ASK HIM TO STOP THIS REVOLT AGAINST US.

YOU ARE RIGHT, SIR. HIS FRIENDSHIP CAN BE AN ASSET TO THE MUGHAL EMPIRE.

RANA PRATAP ENTERED WITH HIS SON, AMAR SINGH.

THAT IS ENOUGH FOR NOW, MINISTER WE WILL DISCUSS THE MATTER LATER. RAJA MAN SINGH MUST BE HUNGRY. LET US OFFER HIM OUR SIMPLE FOOD, AMAR.

YES FATHER!

WON'T YOU JOIN ME?

NO, YOU ARE OUR GUEST. SO, YOU MUST EAT BEFORE US.

BUT THE HOST MUST ALSO EAT WITH THE GUEST.

I AM SORRY, BUT I CAN'T EAT WITH YOU.

MAY I KNOW WHY?

SOON AFTER MAN SINGH LEFT, RANA PRATAP ATTACKED A CAMP OF MUGHAL FORCES AND KILLED MANY OF THEM.

IN THE COURT OF AKBAR—

PRATAP HAS LEFT US NO OTHER ALTERNATIVE. WE WILL HAVE TO CRUSH HIM.

VERY WELL, THEN DO IT.

SOON MAN SINGH AND PRINCE SALIM SET OUT WITH A HUGE ARMY.

IF WE CAN DRIVE PRATAP OUT OF HIS FORT, THEN OUR TASK WILL BECOME EASY.

YES, WITH OUR LARGE ARMY WE CAN DEFEAT HIM.

FINALLY AKBAR'S FORCES REACHED THE FAMOUS BATTLE-GROUND, HALDI-GHATI, SITUATED IN A NARROW VALLEY.

NOW BEGINS THE TOUGHEST PART OF OUR JOB.

MAN SINGH ALSO RECEIVED VITAL INFORMATION.

COMMANDER MAN SINGH, PRATAP HAS ONLY 22,000 SOLDIERS AND THEY HAVE NO GUNS.

THAT IS GOOD NEWS.

THIS MAN PRATAP MUST BE STUPID TO CHALLENGE THE MUGHAL EMPIRE WITHOUT ENOUGH SOLDIERS AND GOOD WEAPONS.

BRAVE, NOT STUPID! HE IS A TRUE RAJPUT AND...

...DON'T BE OVERCONFIDENT, PRINCE. HUGE ARMIES AND GOOD WEAPONS DO HELP IN A BATTLE. BUT WHEN IT COMES TO FIGHTING, THERE IS NO SUBSTITUTE FOR COURAGE.

LET US STOP THIS IDLE CHATTER AND ATTACK.

WE CAN'T.

WHY NOT?

BECAUSE THE WAY TO PRATAP'S FORT LIES THROUGH THAT NARROW VALLEY AND...

...PRATAP'S SOLDIERS ARE WAITING THERE TO TRAP US. WE WILL HAVE TO WAIT FOR THEM TO ATTACK FIRST.

AFTER A LONG WAIT —

WE CAN'T WAIT INDEFINITELY. LET US ATTACK AT ONCE.

NO, PRINCE SALIM!

SIR, I HAVE FOUND A LONG BUT EASY PATH LEADING TO PRATAP'S FORT.

GOOD, TAKE ENOUGH SOLDIERS AND ATTACK THE FORT FROM THE REAR.

YES SIR!

AND A STRONG MUGHAL FORCE MARCHED OFF TO SURROUND RANA PRATAP'S FORT.

WHEN RANA PRATAP HEARD ABOUT THIS NEW TROOP MOVEMENT, HE WAS WORRIED.

THE BEST STRATEGY WOULD HAVE BEEN TO FIGHT FROM THE FORT BUT NOW WE HAVE TO FACE THEM IN HALDI—GHATI.

FINALLY IN THE VALLEY CALLED HALDI-GHATI —

ATTACK!

PRATAP AND HIS SOLDIERS CHARGED FIERCELY.

EVEN PRATAP'S FAITHFUL HORSE CHETAK PARTICIPATED IN THE BATTLE.

THE MUGHAL FORCES SUFFERED HEAVY LOSSES.

BUT JUST WHEN THE MUGHALS STARTED TO LOSE, MORE OF THEIR TROOPS ARRIVED.

IN THE BITTER FIGHTING THAT FOLLOWED, RANA PRATAP LOST 15,000 MEN.

BUT THE BATTLE CONTINUED.

MAN SINGH IS AN ABLE COMMANDER. IF HE IS KILLED, HIS FORCES WILL LOSE THEIR MORALE.

RANA PRATAP ADVANCED TOWARDS MAN SINGH.

MAN SINGH WAS RIDING AN ELEPHANT. PRATAP ATTACKED HIM LIKE A FIERCE LION.

PRATAP THREW HIS SPEAR AT MAN SINGH, BUT JUST THEN THE ELEPHANT MOVED AND PRATAP MISSED HIS MARK. MAN SINGH WAS SAVED.

MEANWHILE PRATAP WAS SURROUNDED BY ENEMY SOLDIERS.

FINDING THEIR LEADER IN DANGER, PRATAP'S FRIEND, MANA AND A FEW SOLDIERS RUSHED TO HIS RESCUE.

OUR RANA IS WOUNDED. I MUST SAVE HIM.

TO SAVE PRATAP, MANA PLACED PRATAP'S HELMET ON HIS OWN HEAD.

THE MUGHAL SOLDIERS WERE FOOLED. THEY ATTACKED MANA, MISTAKING HIM FOR PRATAP. WHILE MANA FACED THE ENEMY, PRATAP WAS CARRIED AWAY BY HIS FAITHFUL HORSE, CHETAK.

SOME RAJPUT SOLDIERS RODE WITH CHETAK TO PROTECT THE UNCONSCIOUS RANA.

THE WOUNDED PRATAP WAS TAKEN TO A CAVE IN THE JUNGLES.

THOUGH PRATAP SURVIVED, HIS FAMILY HAD A HARD TIME. FOR SEVERAL DAYS THEY HAD NOTHING TO EAT BUT WILD BERRIES AND ROOTS.

ONE DAY, WHEN PRATAP'S SON, AMAR SINGH, WAS EATING A DRY CHAPATI...

FATHER, THE CAT SNATCHED MY CHAPATI.

PRATAP'S DAUGHTER, WHO GAVE HER CHAPATI TO HER BROTHER, FAINTED DUE TO HUNGER.

I CAN'T BEAR IT ANY MORE. I SHALL WRITE TO AKBAR.

SOME TIME LATER, IN AKBAR'S COURT —

AT LAST RANA PRATAP HAS DECIDED TO BOW DOWN TO ME. THIS IS AN OCCASION FOR CELEBRATION.

PRITHVIRAJ, A RAJPUT POET IN AKBAR'S COURT, WAS A SECRET ADMIRER OF PRATAP. HE DID NOT LIKE THE NEWS.

SO THE LAST HOPE OF FREEDOM IS ALSO LOST. I MUST DO SOMETHING ABOUT IT.

AND POET PRITHVIRAJ SENT A LETTER TO RANA PRATAP.

You alone can preserve the honour of the Rajputs. The sun would sooner rise in the west than have you address Akbar as your lord.

INSPIRING WORDS! I MUST WRITE TO HIM THAT THE SUN WILL CONTINUE TO RISE IN THE EAST. I WILL NEVER BOW BEFORE AKBAR.

UNAWARE OF PRITHVIRAJ'S LETTER, AKBAR SENT A LARGE BAND OF SOLDIERS TO ESCORT PRATAP FROM THE JUNGLES.

WHEN RANA PRATAP REFUSED TO GO WITH THEM, THE SOLDIERS ATTACKED HIM.

WE ARE GREATLY OUTNUMBERED.

FIGHT, MY BRAVE MEN!

SOON ALL THE RAJPUT SOLDIERS WERE KILLED AND PRATAP WAS ABOUT TO BE CAPTURED, WHEN A BAND OF BHIL TRIBALS ATTACKED THE MUGHALS.

THE BHILS RESCUED PRATAP AND HIS FAMILY AND CARRIED THEM TO THEIR VILLAGE. PRATAP WAS SAD OVER THE LOSS OF HIS SOLDIERS.

EVERYTHING IS FINISHED NOW. I CAN'T LIBERATE MY MOTHER-LAND.

YOU SHOULDN'T LOSE HEART, RANAJI. YOU ARE OUR ONLY HOPE.

BUT WITHOUT AN ARMY HOW CAN I FACE THE MUGHALS?

I WILL COLLECT MY TRIBESMEN FROM THE JUNGLE AND THEN YOU CAN FIGHT AGAIN.

BUT FOR RAISING AN ARMY WE NEED MONEY AND I HAVE NONE.

ONE DAY—

I CAN'T REMAIN A BURDEN ON YOU ANY MORE. I SHALL GO AWAY FROM HERE.

YOU ARE NOT A BURDEN, RANAJI.

JUST THEN A MESSENGER ARRIVED.

RANAJI, A PERSON CALLED BHAMA SHAH WANTS TO MEET YOU.

BRING HIM IN.

RANAJI, I HEARD THAT YOU NEED MONEY. MY WEALTH IS AT YOUR DISPOSAL.

BUT I CAN'T ACCEPT YOUR PERSONAL PROPERTY.

BHAMA SHAH WAS A PROMINENT BUSINESSMAN OF CHITTOR.

NOTHING REMAINS PERSONAL WHEN OUR COUNTRY IS IN TROUBLE. NOW EVERYTHING BELONGS TO THE COUNTRY.

WITH THE HELP OF THIS HUGE WEALTH, PRATAP RAISED A POWERFUL ARMY OF BHILS.

NOW, WE ARE PREPARED TO FIGHT THE MUGHALS AGAIN.

JAI CHANDI! HAR HAR MAHADEV!

PRATAP LED THE BRAVE BHILS TO MANY VICTORIES.

THE FORT OF PHINSAHRA WAS WON FROM THE MUGHALS.

THEN PRATAP SWIFTLY ATTACKED OTHER NEARBY FORTS UNDER MUGHAL OCCUPATION.

FINALLY RANA PRATAP MANAGED TO LIBERATE THE AREAS OF DEVAR, UDAIPUR AND KOMALMIR.

BUT CHITTOR WAS STILL OCCUPIED BY THE MUGHALS. PRATAP HAD FOUGHT RELENTLESSLY FOR TWENTY YEARS. NOW HE WAS VERY SICK.

SOON YOU WOULD BE HEALTHY AGAIN, RANAJI!

NO, I KNOW THAT MY END HAS COME.

HOW UNLUCKY I AM THAT I COULD NOT LIBERATE MY MOTHER-LAND, CHITTOR.

THUS WITH HIS DREAM ONLY PARTIALLY FULFILLED, RANA PRATAP PASSED AWAY. TILL THE LAST DAY OF HIS LIFE, HE STRICTLY ADHERED TO HIS OATH. EVEN WHEN HE WAS SICK, HE DID NOT SLEEP ON A COMFORTABLE BED, BUT ON THE GROUND. THUS RANA PRATAP SET AN EXAMPLE TO LEADERS OF ALL TIMES THAT THEY HAD NO RIGHT TO LIVE IN LUXURY WHEN THE COUNTRY SUFFERED.

RANA SANGA

The route to your roots

RANA SANGA

Rana Sanga, the ruler of Mewar, had his eyes set on the throne of Delhi. However, the rising Mughal star Babur got rid of the Lodhi Sultan of Delhi. Thus the stage was set for the confrontation between the formidable Rana and an equally determined Babur who had just found a new home for his men – Hindustan.

Script
Rajendra Sanjay

Illustrations
Ram Waeerkar

Editor
Anant Pai

Cover illustration by: C.M. Vitankar

RANA SANGA

RANA RAIMAL, WHO RULED MEWAR IN THE EARLY HALF OF THE SIXTEENTH CENTURY, WAS A VALIANT KING WHO UPHELD THE GLORIOUS TRADITIONS OF HIS LAND. HIS THREE SONS, SANGA, PRITHVIRAJ AND JAIMAL, HOWEVER, WERE FOR EVER INVOLVED IN PETTY QUARRELS WITH ONE ANOTHER.

THE DISUNITY OF OUR SONS WILL BE THE RUIN OF OUR KINGDOM.

BUT WHY DO THEY QUARREL SO?

EACH OF THEM WANTS TO BE MY SUCCESSOR.

BUT SANGA, THE ELDEST, HAS THE RIGHT TO THE THRONE.

THAT'S TRUE. THE PRINCES MIGHT HAVE ACCEPTED IT BUT FOR YOUR BROTHER, SURAJMAL. HE SETS THEM AGAINST ONE ANOTHER.

I CAN'T UNDERSTAND WHY HE DOES IT.

WHILE RAIMAL WORRIED, THE PRINCES CONTINUED TO QUARREL AND DRAW THEIR SWORDS AT THE SLIGHTEST PRETEXT.

I AM A BORN LEADER — BORN TO BE THE RULER OF MEWAR.

UNFORTUNATELY I AM THE RIGHTFUL HEIR, PRITHVIRAJ.

RIGHTFUL PERHAPS—BUT YOU ARE NOT FIT TO RULE, SANGA.

WHO SAYS SO?

I DO!

BEFORE SANGA COULD SAY ANYTHING, SURAJMAL CUT IN—

YOU FORGET ONE THING, PRITHVIRAJ— YOU HAVE NOT TAKEN INTO ACCOUNT THE WISHES OF THE PEOPLE.

WHAT CHANCE DO THE WISHES OF THE PEOPLE HAVE AGAINST MY MIGHT?

AS SANGA WAS ABOUT TO REPLY—

LET THE ORACLE, CHARANI DEVI, GUIDE US. HER PREDICTIONS NEVER GO WRONG.

THEY MOUNTED THEIR HORSES...

...AND SOON ARRIVED AT THE TEMPLE OF CHARANI DEVI.

WE HAVE COME TO CONSULT CHARANI DEVI.

WHAT DO YOU WANT TO KNOW?

WE'D LIKE TO KNOW WHICH OF US IS DESTINED TO RULE MEWAR.

PLEASE SIT DOWN. I WILL PUT THE QUESTION TO THE DEVI. SHE WILL GIVE YOU THE ANSWER THROUGH HER ATTENDANT.

SANGA, IF THE PREDICTION IS NOT IN YOUR FAVOUR, WHAT WILL YOU DO?

THE CALM AND PEACE OF THE TEMPLE HAD A STRANGE EFFECT ON SANGA. HE NO LONGER WANTED TO FIGHT WITH HIS BROTHERS.

I WILL GO AWAY AND ESTABLISH A NEW KINGDOM ELSEWHERE, IF MEWAR IS NOT DESTINED TO BE MINE.

AND IF IT IS, YOU WILL HAVE TO KILL ME FIRST.

MEANWHILE, THE PRIEST RETURNED WITH THE ATTENDANT WHO WAS THE MOUTHPIECE OF THE DEVI.

HERE THEY COME— WITH THE PREDICTION!

THE ATTENDANT POINTED TO THE TIGER SKIN ON WHICH SANGA WAS SITTING AND SURAJMAL WAS RESTING A KNEE.

THAT MEANS I AM TO RULE THE KINGDOM...

...OF WHICH I WILL ENJOY A SHARE.

SO THAT WAS THE JACKAL'S GAME!

BRISTLING WITH RAGE, PRITHVIRAJ DREW HIS SWORD AND CHARGED AT SANGA.

I WILL KILL THE LION FIRST AND THEN TACKLE THE JACKAL.

BUT SURAJMAL WHO LEAPT FORWARD TO PARRY THE THRUST...

...RECEIVED THE BLOW.

WHEN SANGA SAW THIS—

I WILL NOT INVOLVE MYSELF IN A FIGHT WITH MY BROTHER—AND CERTAINLY NOT IN THIS TEMPLE.

HE RAN OUT...

...AND MOUNTED HIS HORSE.

STOP SANGA! OR I'LL SHOOT YOU DOWN.

PRITHVIRAJ PULLED OUT AN ARROW AND TOOK AIM.

THE ARROW HIT SANGA IN ONE EYE, BLINDING IT FOR LIFE.

AH!

SANGA, STOP! I SAY STOP.

AT THAT MOMENT, VEEDA, A TRADESMAN WHO WAS PREPARING TO GO OUT OF MEWAR, WAS TAKING LEAVE OF HIS FAMILY. SUDDENLY—

THE PRINCES! THEY ARE COMING THIS WAY.

A FEW SECONDS LATER, UNABLE TO RIDE FURTHER, SANGA CAME TO A HALT IN FRONT OF VEEDA.

PRINCE SANGA! YOU ARE BADLY WOUNDED!

VEEDA HELPED SANGA DISMOUNT AND TURNED TO HIS WIFE—

QUICK! LEAD HIM TO MY HORSE, WHICH IS TIED BEHIND THE HOUSE. I'LL HANDLE JAIMAL.

A FEW SECONDS AFTER VEEDA'S WIFE LED SANGA AWAY, JAIMAL RODE UP.

WHERE IS SANGA?

I'LL GIVE UP MY LIFE BUT I'LL NEVER TELL YOU.

ENRAGED, JAIMAL DREW HIS SWORD AND ATTACKED VEEDA.

THIS SHOULD GIVE PRINCE SANGA ENOUGH TIME TO GET AWAY.

VEEDA STOPPED JAIMAL BUT AT THE COST OF HIS LIFE.

SANGA, MEANWHILE, ESCAPED ON VEEDA'S HORSE.

I WILL NOT GO BACK. PRITHVIRAJ IS DETERMINED TO TAKE THE THRONE. OUR WAR OVER THE SUCCESSION WILL BENEFIT NONE BUT THE ENEMIES OF MEWAR.

SO SANGA RODE AWAY FROM CHITTOR TOWARDS THE JUNGLES.

A FEW HOURS LATER, SANGA SAW SOME SHEPHERDS. HE APPROACHED THEM FOR WORK.

CAN YOU GRAZE OUR GOATS AND SHEEP AND COOK FOR US?

I WILL TRY.

AS A MENIAL, SANGA, THE PRINCE, WAS A FAILURE.

HE IS A GOOD-FOR-NOTHING!

IT'S NO USE KEEPING HIM.

FROM HIS WOUNDS I WOULD SAY HE IS A RUN-AWAY BANDIT.

SANGA SOON BECAME SICK AND TIRED OF THEIR STEADY ABUSE.

I MUST FIND SOME OTHER EMPLOYMENT.

BUT NOTHING CAME HIS WAY.

A FEW DAYS LATER—

ARMED HORSEMEN! THEY SEEM TO BE REBEL RAJPUTS.

WHO ARE YOU?

THEY HAVEN'T RECOGNISED ME. SHALL I ASK THEM TO GIVE ME SOME ARMS?

MY NAME IS SANGRAM SINGH. I TOO AM A RAJPUT. BUT I HAVE NO ARMS EVEN FOR MY OWN PROTECTION.

WE'LL GIVE YOU ARMS. WHY DON'T YOU JOIN US?

WITH PLEASURE!

MY LUCK SEEMS TO HAVE TURNED.

COME, THEN. WE'LL TAKE YOU TO OUR CHIEF.

SANGA WAS INTRODUCED TO THEIR CHIEF, KARAM CHAND.

THIS BRAVE RAJPUT, SANGRAM SINGH, WISHES TO WORK WITH US.

LET'S HOPE YOU MAKE A GOOD DACOIT.

OH! SO THEY'RE REBELS WHO HAVE TURNED DACOITS.

AS SANGA HESITATED, KARAM CHAND'S DAUGHTER CAME OUT—

TAKE SANGRAM IN AND ATTEND TO HIS NEEDS.

YES, FATHER.

SANGA AND KARAM CHAND'S DAUGHTER SOON FELL IN LOVE WITH EACH OTHER. ONE DAY—

WHAT ARE YOU DOING HERE ALONE?

THINKING!

WHAT ARE YOU THINKING ABOUT?

I DO NOT LIKE THE LIFE I'M LEADING.

NEITHER DO I.

THEN WHY DON'T YOU MARRY ME AND COME AWAY WITH ME?

MARU, ONE OF THE REBELS, OVERHEARD THEIR CONVERSATION AND TOLD KARAM CHAND ABOUT IT.

SO SANGRAM HAS NO TASTE FOR OUR WAY OF LIFE. HM.M..!

KARAM CHAND ASKED MARU TO KEEP A CLOSE WATCH ON SANGA. A FEW DAYS LATER—

WHAT IS IT, MARU?

COME OUT AND SEE FOR YOURSELF, SIR. IT'S UNBELIEVABLE!

YES. I AM RANA SANGA. BUT I WANT YOU TO KEEP MY SECRET AND GIVE ME PROTECTION TILL I KNOW WHAT THE SITUATION IS LIKE IN CHITTOR.

WE WILL SEND SOMEONE TO FIND OUT.

THE MESSENGER RETURNED WITH INTERESTING NEWS. SANGA'S BAD DAYS WERE OVER. PRITH- VIRAJ AND JAIMAL WERE NO MORE.

THE KING'S MEN ARE LOOKING FOR YOU EVERYWHERE.

GO TO CHITTOR. DON'T WASTE ANOTHER MOMENT.

MEANWHILE, AT CHITTOR—

TWO SONS KILLED, AND SANGA NOT YET TRACED.

WHO WILL SUCCEED ME? WHAT WILL BECOME OF MY KINGDOM.

HAVE PATIENCE, SIR. OUR MEN ARE LOOKING EVERYWHERE FOR...

18

AT THAT MOMENT—

MAHARAJ KI JAI! PRINCE SANGA IS HERE!

MY SON! WHERE IS MY SON?

WHERE IS HE?

GOD HAS GRANTED OUR PRAYERS!

SON, WHERE WERE YOU ALL THIS TIME?

WHAT DOES IT MATTER? HE IS HERE NOW.

YES. I AM HERE, ALIVE AND WELL!

SOON AFTERWARDS, RAIMAL DIED AND SANGA BECAME KING. WITHIN A FEW YEARS, MEWAR REACHED THE SUMMIT OF PROSPERITY. ONE DAY AT COURT—

IBRAHIM LODI'S POWER IS ALREADY ON THE DECLINE.

WE CAN VANQUISH THE SULTAN WITHOUT MUCH DIFFICULTY!

TO WIN DELHI IS TO RULE THE WHOLE COUNTRY!

SULTAN, I WILL NOT LET YOU ESCAPE!

THE SULTAN WAS SOON CAPTURED.

HIS ARMY HAD FLED.

THOUGH A PRISONER, MAHMOOD KHILJI WAS TREATED LIKE AN HONOURED GUEST.

WHY DO YOU TREAT ME, A PRISONER, SO ROYALLY?

BECAUSE YOU ARE A KING AND A GUEST IN MY PALACE.

I COULD EASILY ESCAPE.

THAT WOULD BE COWARDLY.

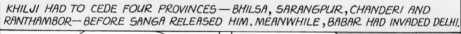

KHILJI HAD TO CEDE FOUR PROVINCES — BHILSA, SARANGPUR, CHANDERI AND RANTHAMBOR — BEFORE SANGA RELEASED HIM. MEANWHILE, BABAR HAD INVADED DELHI.

BABAR IS JUST ANOTHER PLUNDERER!

IF HE DEFEATS LODI, HE WILL COLLECT ALL THE WEALTH HE CAN AND GO BACK!

AND IF HE STAYS ON, IT WON'T MAKE ANY DIFFERENCE TO US.

HIS NEW REGIME WILL NOT BE STRONG ENOUGH TO RESIST US.

WHETHER WE FIGHT LODI OR BABAR — IT IS ALL THE SAME TO US.

WE MUST TAKE OVER DELHI AT ALL COSTS.

IN APRIL 1526, BABAR DEFEATED IBRAHIM LODI, BECAME THE NEW RULER OF DELHI AND IMMEDIATELY MADE PREPARATIONS FOR A WAR ON CHITTOR. SANGA HELD COUNCIL WITH HIS MINISTERS.

AMAZING! BABAR HAS COMPLETED HIS PREPARATIONS!

HE SEEMS TO BE AMBITIOUS.

ALL BRAVE MEN ARE AMBITIOUS. SHILADITYA, OUR FORCES HAVE TO BE FURTHER STRENGTHENED.

HE SHOULD BE DRIVEN OUT OF OUR MOTHERLAND.

I LIKE YOUR SPIRIT, SHILADITYA. I PUT YOU IN CHARGE OF THE DEFENCE UNITS.

WE TRUST YOU TO PERFORM YOUR TASK WITH HONOUR AND SINCERITY.

I WILL NOT HESITATE TO LAY DOWN MY LIFE IN DOING MY DUTY.

MEANWHILE, AT BABAR'S COURT IN DELHI—

JAHANPANAH, WE WILL RUN A GREAT RISK IN FIGHTING RANA SANGA.

OUR SOLDIERS ARE OVERAWED BY THE VALOUR OF THE RAJPUTS.

LET US TEST THE METTLE OF THIS MAN WHO HAS ONLY ONE EYE AND ONE ARM.

IN MARCH 1527, BABAR ATTACKED. THE FORCES OF RANA SANGA AND BABAR MET IN THE BATTLEFIELD OF KHANWA.

BABAR'S ADVANCE OF ABOUT 1500 MEN WAS CUT TO PIECES.

REINFORCEMENTS WERE SENT BUT THEY TOO MADE A HURRIED RETREAT.

JAHANPANAH, OUR SOLDIERS HAVE ALREADY LOST HEART.

I WILL SPEAK TO THEM.

BABAR ORDERED THE DESTRUCTION OF ALL WINE FLASKS.

I VOW NEVER TO DRINK WINE AGAIN.

THEN HE MADE A STIRRING SPEECH BEFORE HIS SOLDIERS.

...BY THE HOLY KORAN, VICTORY WILL BE OURS.

I HOPE I DO NOT HAVE TO SUE FOR PEACE.

ON THE SECOND DAY OF THE BATTLE, HOWEVER, BABAR SENT HIS EMISSARY TO RANA SANGA.

WE WILL ACCEPT BABAR'S PEACE PROPOSAL— ON OUR TERMS.

BUT BABAR REJECTED THE TERMS. A LITTLE LATER—

JEHANPANAH, RANA SANGA'S EMISSARY IS HERE.

BRING HIM IN WITH DUE HONOUR.

ACCEPT OUR TERMS. IT IS NOT POSSIBLE TO DEFEAT SANGA'S ARMY.

YOU CAN MAKE IT POSSIBLE.

WHAT DO YOU MEAN?

IF WE JOIN HANDS, WE CAN BOTH GET WHAT WE WANT!

YOU MEAN YOU WIN THE WAR.

AND YOU GET CHITTOR!

GREED GOT THE BETTER OF SHILADITYA.

YOU WON'T GO BACK ON YOUR WORD, WILL YOU?

ON THE HOLY KORAN — I WILL NOT.

AS SOON AS SHILADITYA RETURNED TO HIS CAMP—

THE RANA HAS BEEN ASKING FOR YOU.

I'LL GO TO HIM.

IS MY SECRET ALREADY KNOWN?

FOR THAT VERY REASON YOU WILL LEAD THE FRONTAL ATTACK, SHILADITYA. I WILL LEAD THE REAR ATTACK.

I WILL ASTONISH YOU WITH MY PROWESS.

I HAVE COMPLETE FAITH IN YOU.

IN THE DARK NIGHT, SANGA LEFT FOR THE HILL WITH HIS TROOPS.

BOTH ARMIES ARE GETTING READY.

MOTHER CHANDI IS MY WITNESS — WE WILL WIN.

THIS WILL BE THE DECISIVE DAY.

THE TWO ARMIES SOON FACED EACH OTHER.

SUDDENLY—

LOOK! LOOK! INSTEAD OF FIGHTING, THE TWO ARMIES ARE MARCHING TOWARDS CHITTOR TOGETHER.

WE HAVE BEEN BETRAYED. SHILADITYA, I TRUSTED YOU...

SINCE THE MAJOR PART OF HIS ARMY HAD BEEN GIVEN TO SHILADITYA, RANA SANGA HAD TO ABANDON HIS PLANS.

A REAR ATTACK WOULD NOW BE IN VAIN.

RANA SANGA AND HIS MEN WANDERED INTO THE HILLS, AWAITING AN OPPORTUNITY TO ATTACK THE MUGHALS.

I VOW NOT TO RETURN TO MEWAR UNTIL I'VE VANQUISHED THE MUGHALS.

WE ARE WITH YOU.

BUT THE UNCERTAINTY AND INSECURITY OF LIFE IN EXILE AFFECTED THE RANA'S HEALTH.

HE WAS CONFINED TO BED AND WAS UNABLE TO FULFIL HIS VOW.

WILL YOU FORGIVE YOUR DEFAULTING SON, O MOTHERLAND?

A FEW MONTHS LATER, HE DIED AT VASVA, A VILLAGE IN THE HILLS.

IF SHILADITYA HAD NOT BETRAYED RANA SANGA, INDIA PERHAPS WOULD HAVE BEEN SAVED THE HUMILIATION OF FOREIGN DOMINATION.